Strawberry Picking

June Crebbin

Illustrated by Peter Kavanagh

 CAMBRIDGE
UNIVERSITY PRESS

Tom wanted to go strawberry picking.

Last summer, all his family had gone strawberry picking – Mum, Dad, his sister Emma, and even Ben his little brother. But not Tom. He had stayed indoors with Grandma because of his hay fever.

The day was hot. Mum was out with Emma, so
Tom asked Dad, "Can we go strawberry picking
today?"

"What about your hay fever?" said Dad.

"It's a lot better now that I'm six," said Tom. "Please let's go. I always miss things."

Dad smiled. "We have to go shopping first, and later we're going to Grandma's for tea. But we might go strawberry picking in between."

Tom almost enjoyed the shopping. They went
to the paper shop, and then to the greengrocer's.
Inside the shop, there were lots of strawberries.

Dad, Ben and Tom went inside and waited in the line. When it was Dad's turn, he said to Tom, "Keep an eye on Ben for me."

Ben wandered off to the other end of the shop. Tom followed. He knew what to do.

YUM YUM!

One of Tom's friends came into the shop.

"Hi, Tom," said his friend. "Do you like my new bike?" He pointed outside.

Tom wanted a new bike. He only had Emma's old one.

He went to look at the bike through the shop window. He and his friend chatted.

Ben looked at the strawberries. He picked one out of a box. He took a big bite, then he put it back.

He picked another strawberry out of another box. He took a big bite and put it back.

He moved along the row of boxes. He took a strawberry from every box. He took a big bite and put it back.

Suddenly, there was a shout. Ben stopped.
Tom stopped. Tom turned round.
Dad was pointing at Ben.

9

"I told you to keep an eye on him," he said.

"I did," said Tom. "He's all right."

"Yes, but he's been eating strawberries!" said Dad.

Dad picked out all the strawberries that Ben had half eaten, and he took them to the shopkeeper to pay for them. He took Ben with him.

On the way home, Tom said, "Dad, I'm sorry about Ben. I didn't see what he was doing."

Dad smiled. "That's OK. We'd better take him proper strawberry picking now."

When they arrived at the strawberry farm,
Dad collected some boxes.

"I want to fill three boxes," said Tom. Emma had
filled three last year.

"Goodness," said Dad. "You'd better get started.
Off you go. I'll keep an eye on Ben."

Tom filled one box. It took a long time and it was very hot. When he had filled two boxes, he sat down for a rest. He could see Dad further down the line, but he couldn't see Ben.

A dry wind blew in his face. The field was
very dusty.

Tom's eyes began to itch. He wanted to rub
them, but he knew that that would make his hay
fever worse. He stood up and carried on picking.

But he had to keep stopping. His eyes were
really stinging now. Tears ran down his cheeks.
The back of his throat was dry.

Quickly, he put down his boxes, turned away,
and sneezed again and again into his handkerchief.

Suddenly, Dad appeared. "Have you seen Ben?"
he said.

"No," said Tom.

"I can't find him," said Dad. "I took my eyes off
him for one minute and now he's gone."

They both went to look for him. They walked
up and down the rows of strawberry pickers.
They asked people if they had seen a little boy.
But no-one had.

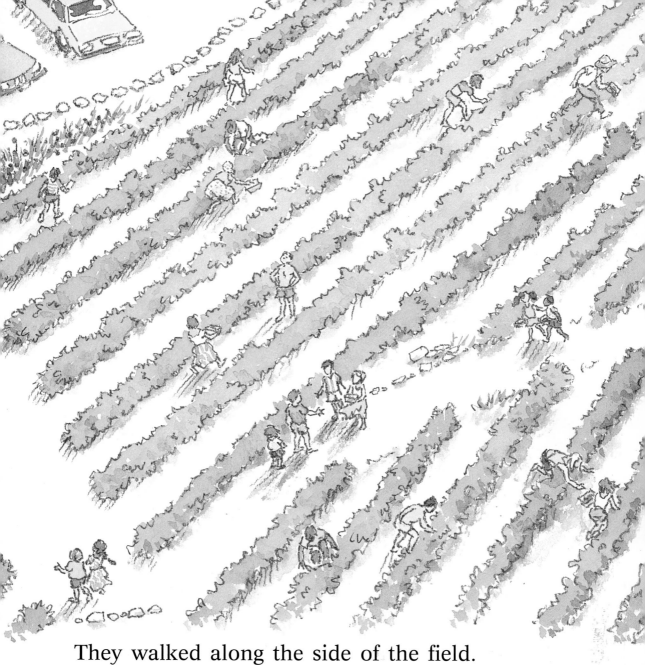

They walked along the side of the field.
Then they found him, fast asleep under a tree.
"Thank goodness," said Dad, picking him up.
"I think it's time to go."

"But I want to fill this last box," said Tom.

"Oh dear," said Dad, looking at him. "Your hay fever *is* bad, isn't it?"

"I'm OK, Dad."

Tom went off to fill his last box.

Then they went to Grandma's house.

"Tea's all ready," she said. "There's a special treat today."

She brought in a big dish.

"And we've brought *you* a special treat," said
Tom. He held out a box of strawberries.

Then he looked inside the dish.
"Strawberries!" said Tom.
"Snap!" said everyone.